HISTORY OF THE GOLDEN

It has been said that, as a group, retrievers offer more to dog owners the world over than almost any other kind of dog. Retrievers' attributes range from "baby sitting" to extraordinary powers in retrieving game for hunters.

The three most popular retrievers in the United States at the moment are the Labrador Retriever, Golden Retriever and Chesapeake Bay Retriever. In other parts of the world the relative ranking of the different Retriever breeds—in fact,

The Golden Retriever ranks as one of the most popular of all retrievers.

even the breeds themselves, as not every English-speaking country recognizes the same breeds in all cases—is of course different to account for local tastes and fashions, but in general it is safe to say that retrievers always have a large following.

Retrievers are strong and powerful, muscular and swift of stride. It is remarkable that dogs possessing those characteristics are also gentle with children and mindful of correct etiquette in the home while responding quickly to instructions whether it be for "tricks" or hunting in the field.

The Golden Retriever enjoys a rather unique introduction to the shooting field. In the year 1860, Sir Dudley Majoribanks visited a circus in Brighton, England, and saw the immediate ancestors of the Golden.

The circus was featuring a troop of Russian performing dogs. The feats accomplished by these dogs impressed him so much, that after the show he approached the Russian trainer and tried to purchase a pair of them. The trainer refused to sell a pair, on the grounds that it would spoil his act. Sir Dudley, however, had been so impressed by the performance of these dogs and their intelligence that he made an offer for the entire troop of eight. The trainer accepted and the deal was accomplished. This proved a

The breed's rich, lustrous golden coat is no doubt the source of its name.

fortunate purchase, for he now had enough stock and variety of bloodlines to try some extensive breeding.

These dogs were called Russian Trackers. They came from a very old breed that had served the usual variety of purposes in its original home in Asiatic Russia. One of the chief uses of the Russian Tracker was as a guardian for flocks of sheep, and he was admirably suited to withstand the rigors of the severe winters in the Caucasus Mountains where he made his home.

The Russian Tracker was a much larger dog than his descendant, the Golden Retriever. The original breed measured 30 inches at the shoulder and often weighed as much as 100 pounds.

Today, the males weigh from 65 to 75 pounds, the bitches from 55 to 65 pounds. Sir Dudley established these dogs at his Scottish seat in the Guisachan deer forest in Inverness-shire, Scotland. He bred the dogs without outcrossing for ten years. As the original eight dogs were much larger than the present Golden Retriever, many sportsmen considered them too cumbersome, so around 1870 Sir Dudley decided to try an outcross with the Bloodhound. As far as is known, this is the only cross perpetuated, and this only once. This reduced the breed to its present size, increased the scenting powers, and developed a more refined texture of coat, slightly darker in color.

DESCRIPTION OF THE BREED

The standard of a breed is the criterion by which the appearance (and to a certain extent, the temperament) of any given dog is made subject, as far as possible, to objective measurement. Basically the standard for any breed is a definition of the perfect dog, to which all specimens of the breed are compared; the degree of excellence of the appearance of a given dog for conformation show purposes is in direct proportion to the dog's agreement with the requirements of the standard for its breed. Necessarily, of course, a certain amount of subjective evaluation is involved because of the wording of the standard itself and because of the factors introduced through the agency of the completely human judging apparatus. Breed standards are always subject to change through review by the national breed club for each dog, so it is always wise to keep up with developments in a breed by checking the publications of your national kennel club.

The following is a version of the standard for the Golden Retriever.

THE BREED STANDARD
General appearance: A symmetrical, powerful, active dog, sound and well put together, not clumsy nor long in the leg,

Primarily a hunting dog, the Golden should always be in hard working condition.

displaying a kindly expression and possessing a personality that is eager, alert and self-confident. Primarily a hunting dog, he should be shown in hard working condition. Over-all appearance, balance, gait and purpose to be given more emphasis than any of his component parts.

Head: Broad in skull, slightly arched laterally and longitudinally without prominence of frontal bones (forehead) or occipital bones. Stop well defined but not abrupt. Foreface deep and wide, nearly as long as skull. Muzzle straight in profile, blending smoothly and strongly into skull; when viewed in profile or from above, slightly deeper and wider at stop than at tip. No heaviness in flews. Removal of whiskers is permitted but not preferred.

Eyes: Friendly and intelligent in expression, medium large with dark, close-fitting rims, set well apart and reasonably deep in sockets. Color preferably dark

brown; medium brown acceptable. Slant eyes and narrow, triangular eyes detract from correct expression and are to be faulted. No white or haw visible when looking straight ahead. Dogs showing evidence of functional abnormality of eyelids or eyelashes (such as, but not limited to, trichiasis, entropion, ectropion, or distichiasis) are to be excused from the ring.

Teeth: Scissors bite, in which the outer side of the lower incisors touches the inner side of the upper incisors. Undershot or overshot bite is a disqualification. Misalignment of teeth (irregular placement of incisors) or a level bite (incisors meet each other edge to edge) is undesirable, but not to be confused with undershot or overshot. Full dentition. Obvious gaps are serious faults.

Nose: Black or brownish black, though fading to a lighter shade in cold weather not serious. Pink nose or one seriously lacking in pigmentation to be faulted.

Ears: Rather short with front edge attached well behind and just above the eye and falling close to cheek. When pulled forward, tip of ear should just cover the eye. Low, hound-like ear set to be faulted.

Neck: Medium long, merging gradually into well laid back shoulders, giving sturdy, muscular appearance. Untrimmed natural ruff. No throatiness.

Body: Well-balanced, short coupled, deep through the chest. Chest between forelegs at least as wide as a man's closed hand including thumb, with well-

Inadequate skull for long muzzle. Ears too large, long and curling like that of a hound. Eyes too open and large, with "droopy" lids; poor expression. Drawing by John Quinn.

The eyes of the Golden Retriever should be friendly and intelligent in expression and dark brown in color.

developed forechest. Brisket extends to elbow. Ribs long and well sprung but not barrel shaped, extending well towards hindquarters. Loin short, muscular, wide and deep, with very little tuckup. Back line strong and level from withers to slightly sloping croup, whether standing or moving. Slab-sidedness, narrow chest, lack of depth in brisket, sloping back line, roach or sway back, excessive tuckup, flat or steep croup to be faulted.

Forequarters: Muscular, well coordinated with hindquarters and capable of free movement. Shoulder blades long and well laid back with upper tips fairly close together at withers. Upper arms appear about the same length as the blades, setting the elbows back beneath the upper tip of the

Front too wide, feet turned in. Such a dog will move clumsily. Drawing by John R. Quinn.

Bowed rear. The opposite of cowhocks, but no less a fault even though less common. The tail is ringed (faulty), lessening its usefulness. Drawing by John Quinn.

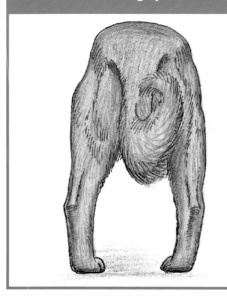

blades, close to the ribs without looseness. Legs, viewed from the front, straight with good bone, but not to the point of coarseness. Pasterns short and strong, sloping slightly with no suggestion of weakness.

Hindquarters: Broad and strongly muscled. Profile of croup slopes slightly; the pelvic bones at a slightly greater angle (approximately 30 degrees from horizontal). In a natural stance, the femur joins the pelvis at approximately a 90-degree angle; stifles well bent; hocks well let down with short, strong rear pasterns. Legs straight when viewed from rear. Cow hocks, spread hocks, and sickle hocks to be faulted.

Feet: Medium size, round, compact, and well knuckled, with thick pads. Excess hair may be trimmed to show natural size and contour. Dewclaws on forelegs may be removed, but are normally left on. Splayed or hare feet to be faulted.

Tail: Well set on, thick and close to body; may be straight or wavy. Moderate feathering on back of forelegs and on underbody; heavier feathering on front of neck, back of thighs and underside of tail. Coat on head,

The Golden Retriever has moderate feathering on the back of the forelegs and on the underbody, and heavier feathering on the front of the neck, back of the thighs and the tail. The coat on the head, paws, and the front of legs is short and even.

muscular at the base, following the natural line of the croup. Tail bones extend to, but not below, the point of hock. Carried with merry action, level or with some moderate upward curve; never curled over back nor between legs.

Coat: Dense and water repellent with good undercoat. Outer coat firm and resilient, neither coarse nor silky, lying paws, and front of legs is short and even. Excessive length, open coats, and limp, soft coats are very undesirable. Feet may be trimmed and stray hairs neatened, but the natural appearance of coat or outline should not be altered by cutting or clipping.

Color: Rich, lustrous golden of various shades. Feathering may be lighter than rest of coat. With

TAIL
Carried level,
heavily feathered.

BACK
Strong and level.

HINDQUARTERS
Broad and muscular.

PASTERN
Strong.

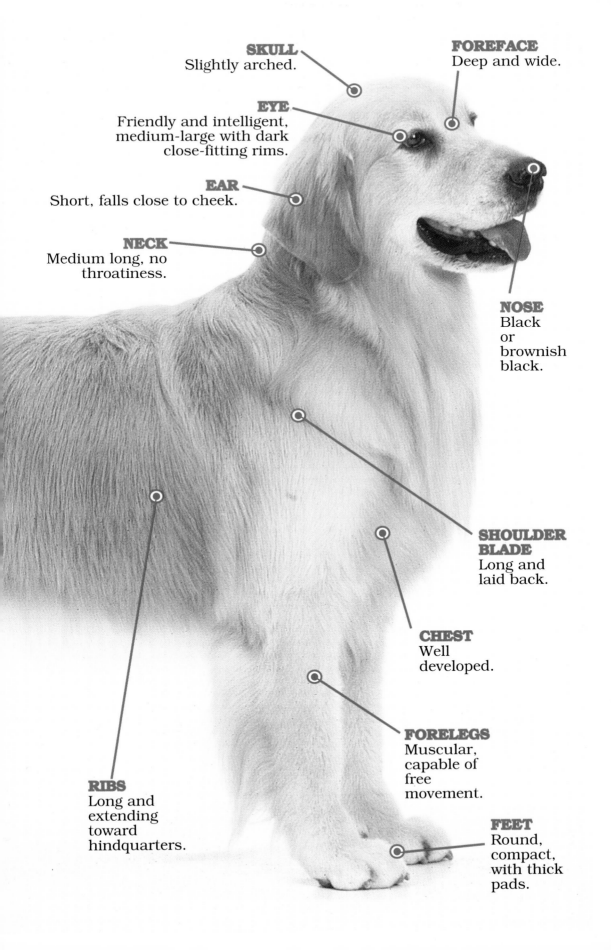

SKULL
Slightly arched.

FOREFACE
Deep and wide.

EYE
Friendly and intelligent,
medium-large with dark
close-fitting rims.

EAR
Short, falls close to cheek.

NECK
Medium long, no
throatiness.

NOSE
Black
or
brownish
black.

**SHOULDER
BLADE**
Long and
laid back.

CHEST
Well
developed.

RIBS
Long and
extending
toward
hindquarters.

FORELEGS
Muscular,
capable of
free
movement.

FEET
Round,
compact,
with thick
pads.

the exception of greying or whitening of face or body due to age, any white marking, other than a few white hairs on the chest, should be penalized according to its extent. Allowable light shadings are not to be confused with white markings. Predominant body color which is either extremely pale or extremely dark is undesirable. Some latitude should be given to the light puppy whose coloring shows promise of deepening with maturity. Any noticeable area of black or other off-color hair is a serious fault.

Gait: When trotting, gait is free, smooth, powerful, and well coordinated, showing good reach. Viewed from any position, legs turn neither in nor out, nor do feet cross or interfere with each other. As speed increases, feet tend to converge toward center line of balance. It is recommended that dogs be shown on a loose lead to reflect true gait.

Size: Males 23-24 inches in height at withers; females 21^1/$_2$-

The Golden Retriever's gait is smooth, powerful, and well coordinated.

22 ^{1}/$_2$ inches. Dogs up to one inch above or below standard size should be proportionately penalized. Deviation in height of more than one inch from the standard shall disqualify. Length from breastbone to point of buttocks slightly greater than height at withers in ratio of 12:11. Weight for dogs 65-75 pounds; bitches 55-65 pounds.

Temperament: Friendly, reliable, and trustworthy. Quarrelsomeness or hostility towards other dogs or people in normal situation, or an unwarranted show of timidity or nervousness, is not in keeping with Golden Retriever character. Such actions should be penalized according to their significance.

Faults: Any departure from the described ideal shall be considered faulty to the degree to which it interferes with the breed's purpose or is contrary to breed character.

Disqualifications: Deviation in height of more than one inch from standard either way.

YOUR NEW GOLDEN PUPPY

SELECTION

When you do pick out a Golden Retriever puppy as a pet, don't be hasty; the longer you study puppies, the better you will understand them. Make it your transcendent concern to select only one that radiates good health and spirit and is lively on his feet, whose eyes are bright, whose coat shines, and who comes forward eagerly to make and to cultivate your acquaintance. Don't fall for any shy little darling that wants to retreat to his bed or his box, or plays coy behind other puppies or people, or hides his head under your arm or jacket appealing to your protective instinct. *Pick the Golden Retriever puppy who forthrightly picks you! The feeling of attraction should be mutual!*

All Golden puppies are adorable, which makes it so hard to choose one. Pick the puppy that picks you!

DOCUMENTS

Now, a little paper work is in order. When you purchase a purebred Golden Retriever puppy, you should receive a transfer of ownership, registration material, and other "papers" (a list of the immunization shots, if any, the puppy may have been given; a note on whether or not the puppy has been wormed; a diet and feeding schedule to which the puppy is accustomed) and you are welcomed as a fellow owner to a long, pleasant association with a most lovable pet, and more (news)paper work.

GENERAL PREPARATION

You have chosen to own a particular Golden Retriever puppy. You have chosen it very carefully over all other breeds and all other puppies. So before you ever get that Golden Retriever puppy home, you will have prepared for its arrival by reading everything you can get your hands on having to do with the management of Golden Retrievers and puppies. True, you will run into many conflicting opinions, but at least you will not be starting "blind." Read, study, digest. Talk over your plans with your veterinarian, other "Golden Retriever people," and the seller of your Golden Retriever puppy.

When you get your Golden

Retriever puppy, you will find that your reading and study are far from finished. You've just scratched the surface in your plan to provide the greatest possible comfort and health for your Golden Retriever; and, by the same token, you do want to assure yourself of the greatest possible enjoyment of this wonderful creature. You must be ready for this puppy mentally as well as in the physical requirements.

TRANSPORTATION

If you take the puppy home by car, protect him from drafts, particularly in cold weather.

Crates are useful when house-breaking your Golden Retriever puppy. The dog's natural instinct is to never soil his sleeping area.

Wrapped in a towel and carried in the arms or lap of a passenger, the Golden Retriever puppy will usually make the trip without mishap. If the pup starts to drool and to squirm, stop the car for a few minutes. Have newspapers handy in case of car-sickness. A covered carton lined with newspapers provides protection for puppy and car, if you are driving alone. Avoid excitement and unnecessary handling of the puppy on arrival. A Golden Retriever puppy is a very small "package" to be making a complete change of surroundings and company, and he needs frequent rest and refreshment to renew his vitality.

THE FIRST DAY AND NIGHT

When your Golden Retriever puppy arrives in your home, put him down on the floor and don't pick him up again, except when it is absolutely necessary. He is a dog, a real dog, and must not be lugged around like a rag doll. Handle him as little as possible, and permit no one to pick him up and baby him. To repeat, *put your Golden Retriever puppy on the floor or the ground and let him stay there except when it may be necessary to do otherwise.*

Quite possibly your Golden Retriever puppy will be afraid for a while in his new surroundings, without his mother and littermates. Comfort him and reassure him, but don't console him. Don't give him the "oh-you-poor-itsy-bitsy-puppy" treatment. Be calm, friendly, and reassuring. Encourage him to walk around

Choose a Golden Retriever puppy whose eyes are bright and whose coat shines.

and sniff over his new home. If it's dark, put on the lights. Let him roam for a few minutes while you and everyone else concerned sit quietly or go about your routine business. Let the puppy come back to you.

Playmates may cause an immediate problem if the new Golden Retriever puppy is to be greeted by children or other pets. If not, you can skip this subject. The natural affinity between puppies and children calls for some supervision until a live-and-let-live relationship is established. This applies particularly to a Christmas puppy, when there is more excitement than usual and more chance for a puppy to swallow something upsetting. It is a better plan to welcome the puppy several days before or after the holiday week. Like a baby, your Golden Retriever puppy needs much rest and should not be over-handled. Once a child realizes that a puppy has "feelings" similar to his own, and can readily be hurt or injured, the opportunities for play and responsibilities provide exercise and training for both.

For his first night with you, he should be put where he is to sleep every night—say in the kitchen, since its floor can usually be easily cleaned. Let him explore the

Your Golden puppy should have a crate, lined with a soft blanket, and plenty of safe toys to satisfy his chewing needs. This puppy is enjoying his Chooz® treat.

As your Golden puppy grows, he will need to learn what is acceptable to chew on and what is not. This Gumabone® is the perfect choice for constructive chewing.

kitchen to his heart's content; close doors to confine him there. Prepare his food and feed him lightly the first night. Give him a pan with some water in it—not a lot, since most puppies will try to drink the whole pan dry. Give him an old coat or shirt to lie on. Since a coat or shirt will be strong in human scent, he will pick it out to lie on, thus furthering his feeling of security in the room where he has just been fed.

HOUSEBREAKING HELPS

Now, sooner or later—mostly sooner—your new Golden puppy is going to "puddle" on the floor. First take a newspaper and lay it on the puddle until the urine is soaked up onto the paper. *Save this paper.* Now take a cloth with soap and water, wipe up the floor and dry it well. Then take the wet paper and place it on a fairly large square of newspapers in a convenient corner. When cleaning up, always keep a piece of wet paper on top of the others. Every time he wants to "squat," he will seek out this spot and use the papers. (This routine is rarely necessary for more than three days.) Now leave your Golden Retriever puppy for the night. Quite probably he will cry and howl a bit; some are more stubborn than others on this matter. But let him stay alone for the night. This may seem harsh treatment, but it is the best procedure in the long run. Just let him cry; he will weary of it sooner or later.

With proper nutrition, exercise, and grooming, your Golden puppy will grow into a strong and healthy adult.

FEEDING

Now let's talk about feeding your Golden Retriever, a subject so simple that it's amazing there is so much nonsense and misunderstanding about it. Is it expensive to feed a Golden Retriever? No, it is not! You can feed your Golden Retriever economically and keep him in perfect shape the year round, or you can feed him expensively. He'll thrive either way, and let's see why this is true.

First of all, remember a Golden Retriever is a dog. Dogs do not have a high degree of selectivity in their food, and unless you spoil them with great variety (and possibly turn them into poor,"picky" eaters) they will eat almost anything that they become accustomed to. Many dogs flatly refuse to eat nice, fresh beef. They pick around it and eat everything else. But meat—bah! Why? They aren't accustomed to it! They'd eat rabbit fast enough, but they refuse beef because they aren't used to it.

VARIETY NOT NECESSARY

A good general rule of thumb is

The basic diet most often recommended for your Golden Retriever is a high-quality dry food, in either meal or kibble form.

Golden Retrievers have hearty appetites. Be sure to keep your food out of your Golden's reach—or he might run off with your lunch!

DOG FOOD

There are almost as many right diets as there are dog experts, but the basic diet most often recommended is one that consists of a dry food, either meal or kibble form. There are several of excellent quality, manufactured by reliable companies, research tested, and nationally advertised. They are inexpensive, highly satisfactory, and easily available in stores everywhere in containers of five to 50 pounds. Larger amounts cost less per pound, usually.

If you have a choice of brands, it is usually safer to choose the better known one; but even so, carefully read the analysis on the package. Do not choose any food in which the protein level is less than 25 percent, and be sure that this protein comes from both animal and vegetable sources. The good dog foods have meat meal, fish meal, liver, and such, plus protein from alfalfa and soybeans, as well as some dried-milk product. Note the vitamin content carefully. See that they are all there in good proportions; and be especially certain that the food contains properly high levels of vitamins A and D, two of the most perishable and important ones. Note the B-complex level, but don't worry about carbohydrate and mineral levels. These substances are plentiful and cheap and not likely to be lacking in a good brand.

forget all human preferences and don't give a thought to variety. Choose the right diet for your Golden Retriever and feed it to him day after day, year after year, winter and summer. But what is the right diet?

Hundreds of thousands of dollars have been spent in canine nutrition research. The results are pretty conclusive, so you needn't go into a lot of experimenting with trials of this and that every other week. Research has proven just what your dog needs to eat and to keep healthy.

Your Golden Retriever will appreciate a tasty treat from time to time.

Vitamins and minerals are naturally present in all the foods; and to ensure against any loss through processing, they are added in concentrated form to the dog food you use. Except on the advice of your veterinarian, extra and added amounts of vitamins can prove harmful to your Golden Retriever! The same risk goes with minerals.

FEEDING SCHEDULE

When and how much food to give your Golden Retriever? As to when (except in the instance of puppies), suit yourself. You may feed two meals per day or the same amount in one single

The advice given for how to choose a dry food also applies to moist or canned types of dog foods, if you decide to feed one of these.

Having chosen a really good food, feed it to your Golden Retriever as the manufacturer directs. And once you've started, stick to it. Never change if you can possibly help it. A switch from one meal or kibble-type food can usually be made without too much upset; however, a change will almost invariably give you (and your Golden Retriever) some trouble.

WHEN SUPPLEMENTS ARE NEEDED

Now what about supplements of various kinds, mineral and vitamin, or the various oils? They are all okay to add to your Golden Retriever's food. However, if you are feeding your Golden Retriever a correct diet, and this is easy to do, no supplements are necessary unless your Golden Retriever has been improperly fed, has been sick, or is having puppies.

Your Golden Retriever should always have access to clean, fresh water, especially when outdoors.

The Plaque Attacker™ from Nylabone® will keep your Golden's teeth clean and free from disease.

growth of the permanent teeth under the puppy teeth, to assist in getting rid of the puppy teeth at the proper time, to help the permanent teeth through the gums, to ensure normal jaw development, and to settle the permanent teeth solidly in the jaws.

The adult Golden Retriever's desire to chew stems from the instinct for tooth cleaning, gum massage, and jaw exercise—plus the need for an outlet for periodic doggie tensions.

This is why dogs, especially puppies and young dogs, will often destroy property worth hundreds of dollars when their chewing instinct is not diverted from their owner's possessions. And this is why you should

feeding, either morning or night. As to how to prepare the food and how much to give, it is generally best to follow the directions on the food package. Your own Golden Retriever may want a little more or a little less.

Fresh, cool water should always be available to your Golden Retriever. This is important to good health throughout his lifetime.

ALL GOLDEN RETRIEVERS NEED TO CHEW

Puppies and young Golden Retrievers need something with resistance to chew on while their teeth and jaws are developing—for cutting the puppy teeth, to induce

The Gumabone® products not only will keep your dog's teeth in top hygienic condition, but they're fun to play with too!

provide your Golden Retriever with something to chew—something that has the necessary functional qualities, is desirable from the Golden Retriever's viewpoint, and is safe for him.

It is very important that your Golden Retriever not be permitted to chew on anything he can break or on any indigestible thing from which he can bite sizable chunks. Sharp pieces, such as from a bone which can be broken by a dog, may pierce the intestinal wall and

commercially in pet stores—may serve your Golden Retriever's teething needs if his mouth is large enough to handle them effectively. You may be tempted to give your Golden Retriever puppy a smaller bone and he may not be able to break it when you do, but puppies grow rapidly and the power of their jaws constantly increases until maturity. This means that a growing Golden Retriever may break one of the smaller bones at any time,

Your Golden should never leave home without a supply of Nylabone® products.

kill. Indigestible things that can be bitten off in chunks, such as from shoes or rubber or plastic toys, may cause an intestinal stoppage (if not regurgitated) and bring painful death, unless surgery is promptly performed.

Strong natural bones, such as 4- to 8-inch lengths of round shin bone from mature beef—either the kind you can get from a butcher or one of the variety available

swallow the pieces, and die painfully before you realize what is wrong.

All hard natural bones are very abrasive. If your Golden Retriever is an avid chewer, natural bones may wear away his teeth prematurely; hence, they then should be taken away from your dog when the teething purposes have been served. The badly worn, and usually painful, teeth of many mature dogs can be traced to excessive chewing on natural bones.

Contrary to popular belief, knuckle bones that can be chewed up and swallowed by your Golden Retriever provide little, if any, usable calcium or other nutriment. They do, however, disturb the digestion of most dogs and cause them to vomit the nourishing food they need.

Dried rawhide products of various types, shapes, sizes, and prices are available on the market and have become quite popular.

However, they don't serve the primary chewing functions very well; they are a bit messy when wet from mouthing, and most Golden Retrievers chew them up rather rapidly—but they have been considered safe for dogs until recently. Now, more and more incidents of death, and near death, by strangulation have been reported to be the results of partially swallowed chunks of

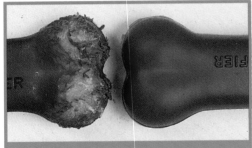

Chocolate Nylabone® has a one micron thickness coat of chocolate under the skin of the nylon. When the Golden Retriever chews it the white surface is exposed. This photo shows before and after chewing.

rawhide swelling in the throat. More recently, some veterinarians have been attributing cases of acute constipation to large pieces of incompletely digested rawhide in the intestine.

A new product, molded rawhide, is very safe. During the process, the rawhide is melted and then injection molded into the familiar dog shape. It is very hard and is eagerly accepted by Golden Retrievers. The melting process also sterilizes the rawhide. Don't confuse this with pressed rawhide, which is nothing more than small strips of rawhide squeezed together.

The nylon bones, especially those with natural meat and bone fractions added, are probably the most complete, safe, and economical answer to the chewing need. Dogs cannot break them or bite off sizable chunks; hence, they are completely safe—and being longer lasting than other things offered for the purpose, they are economical.

Hard chewing raises little bristle-like projections on the

Pet shops sell treats that are healthy and nutritious. Cheese is added to chicken meal, rawhide and other high-protein feeds to be melted together and molded into hard chew devices or pacifiers. Don't waste your money on low-protein treats. If the protein content isn't at least 50% pass it up!

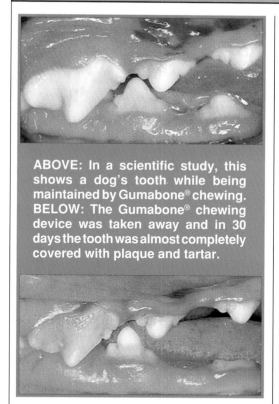

ABOVE: In a scientific study, this shows a dog's tooth while being maintained by Gumabone® chewing. BELOW: The Gumabone® chewing device was taken away and in 30 days the tooth was almost completely covered with plaque and tartar.

Nylabone® is highly recommended by veterinarians as a safe, healthy nylon bone that can't splinter or chip. Nylabone® is frizzled by the dog's chewing action, creating a toothbrush-like surface that cleanses the teeth and massages the gums. Nylabone® pacifiers, the only chew products made of flavor-impregnated solid nylon, are available in your local pet shop. Nylabone® is superior to the cheaper bones because it is made of virgin nylon, which is the strongest and longest-lasting type of nylon available. The cheaper

surface of the nylon bones—to provide effective interim tooth cleaning and vigorous gum massage, much in the same way your toothbrush does it for you. The little projections are raked off and swallowed in the form of thin shavings, but the chemistry of the nylon is such that they break down in the stomach fluids and pass through without effect.

The toughness of the nylon provides the strong chewing resistance needed for important jaw exercise and effectively aids teething functions, but there is no tooth wear because nylon is non-abrasive. Being inert, nylon does not support the growth of microorganisms; and it can be washed in soap and water or it can be sterilized by boiling or in an autoclave.

The nylon tug toy is actually a dental floss. You grab one end and let your Golden tug on the other as it slowly slips through his teeth since nylon is self-lubricating. Do not use cotton rope tug toys as cotton is organic and rots. It is also weak and easily loses strands which are indigestible should the dog swallow them.

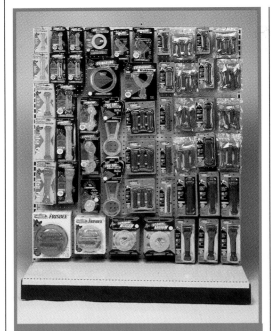

Most pet shops have complete walls dedicated to safe pacifiers.

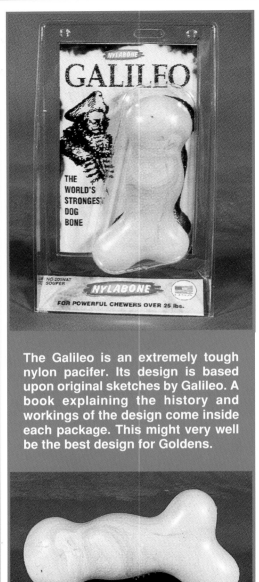

The Galileo is an extremely tough nylon pacifer. Its design is based upon original sketches by Galileo. A book explaining the history and workings of the design come inside each package. This might very well be the best design for Goldens.

bones are made from recycled or re-ground nylon scraps, and have a tendency to break apart and split easily.

Nothing, however, substitutes for periodic professional attention for your Golden Retriever's teeth and gums, not any more than your toothbrush can do that for you. Have your Golden Retriever's teeth cleaned at least once a year by your veterinarian (twice a year is better) and he will be happier, healthier, and far more pleasant to live with.

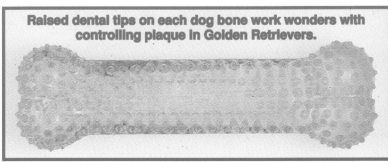

Raised dental tips on each dog bone work wonders with controlling plaque in Golden Retrievers.

Only get the largest plaque attacker for your Golden.

GROOMING

If you keep your dog in the best possible condition at all times, he will not only look his best, but he will feel his best, too. Since the Golden Retriever is a naturally sanitary dog, your problems will be small ones. All your grooming tasks will be easier if you make them fun for both you and the dog. Play with him and talk to him while you are brushing him, bathing him, or trimming his nails. Continually shouting and scolding your dog for not standing still will only make you irritable and the dog shy of grooming.

Grooming your Golden Retriever from an early age will accustom him to this routine early in life. This will make grooming sessions easier on both you and your Golden.

Since grooming can be pleasant and beneficial for both you and your pet, you should try to spend a few moments each day brushing him. For the long-haired Golden use a large metal comb on his coat first; then brush him vigorously with a wire glove or brush. Your pet shop sells both these items, as well as all the other grooming aids you will need. During the shedding seasons in the spring and fall, you will have to spend a little extra time getting loose hair from his coat. Bathe your Golden Retriever no more

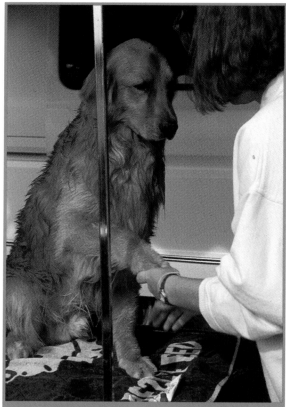

Your Golden Retriever's nails must be checked during every grooming session.

several large towels. Do not turn him loose until you are certain that he is quite dry. He can catch cold easily out in the cool air with a damp coat. He may try to help you dry him by giving himself a good shaking and letting the water fly everywhere. It may seem funny to worry about cold after a bath when discussing breeds like the retrievers who plunge into icy waters to retrieve ducks in mid-winter; however, under the latter circumstances the vigorous exercise and excitement combines to maintain the body temperature. Bathing a passive dog in warm water and then allowing him to remain damp, possibly in a draft, is a far different matter and may very well contribute to a cold.

frequently than he needs to be. Use one of the soaps made especially for dogs. Wash his head first, using a wash cloth. Clean his ears thoroughly (and be sure to dry them thoroughly afterwards). Caution: Do not let water run down into his ears. Never probe into a dog's ears any further than you can see. Be very careful not to get soapy water in his eyes. This won't do permanent damage to his eyes, but it will be very uncomfortable for him and he will resist bathing in the future.

After you have washed and rinsed his head, scrub his body thoroughly, then dry him with

A conditioning shampoo will help to keep your Golden's coat looking its best. Photo courtesy of Hagen.

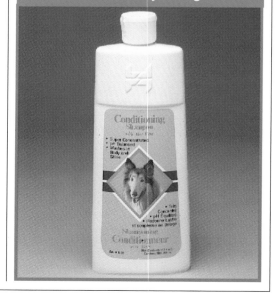

TRAINING

You owe proper training to your Golden Retriever. The right and privilege of being trained is his birthright; and whether your Golden Retriever is going to be a command just as fast; he must walk quietly at "Heel," whether on or off lead. He must be mannerly and polite wherever he goes; he must be polite to strangers on the

Your Golden Retriever puppy is full of playful energy. It is best to channel that energy into learning basic obedience as early as possible.

handsome, well-mannered housedog and companion, a show dog, or whatever possible use he may be put to, the basic training is always the same—all must start with basic obedience, or what might be called "manner training."

Your Golden Retriever must come instantly when called and obey the "Sit" or "Down" street and in stores. He must be mannerly in the presence of other dogs. He must not bark at children on roller skates, motorcycles, or other domestic animals. And he must be restrained from chasing cats. It is not a dog's inalienable right to chase cats, and he must be reprimanded for it.

ABOVE: Close to 50 percent of all service dogs are Golden Retrievers. BELOW: Here a Golden Retriever at seven months of age is being trained as a service dog.

PROFESSIONAL TRAINING

How do you go about this training? Well, it's a very simple procedure, pretty well standardized by now. First, if you can afford the extra expense, you may send your Golden Retriever to a professional trainer, where in 30 to 60 days he will learn how to be a "good dog." If you enlist the services of a good professional trainer, follow his advice of when to come to see the dog. No, he won't forget you, but too-frequent visits at the wrong time may slow down his training progress. And using a "pro" trainer means that you will have to go for some training, too, after the trainer feels your Golden Retriever is ready to go home. You will have to learn how your Golden Retriever works, just what to expect of him

Obedience training is easy for Goldens to learn—they just love to please their master. This dog is learning the "Down/Stay" command.

and how to use what the dog has learned after he is home.

OBEDIENCE TRAINING CLASS

Another way to train your Golden Retriever (many experienced Golden Retriever people think this is the best) is to join an obedience training class right in your own community. There is such a group in nearly every community nowadays. Here you will be working with a group of people who are also just starting out. You will actually be training your own dog, since all work is done under the direction of a head trainer who will make suggestions to you and also tell you when and how to correct your Golden Retriever's errors. Then, too, working with such a group, your Golden Retriever will learn to get along with other dogs. And, what is more important, he will learn to do exactly what he is told to do, no matter how much confusion there is around him or how great the temptation is to go his own way.

Write to your national kennel club for the location of a training club or class in your locality. Sign up. Go to it regularly—every session! Go early and leave late! Both you and your Golden Retriever will benefit tremendously.

This Golden puppy is jumping for joy. He just can't wait for his next training session.

TRAIN HIM BY THE BOOK

The third way of training your Golden Retriever is by the book. Yes, you can do it this way and do a good job of it too. But in using the book method, select a book, buy it, study it carefully; then study it some more, until the procedures are almost second nature to you. Then start your training. But stay with the book and its advice and exercises. Don't start in and then make up a few rules of your own. If you don't follow the book, you'll get into jams you can't get out of by yourself. If after a few hours of short training sessions your Golden Retriever is still not working as he should, get back to the book for a study session, because it's your fault, not the dog's! The procedures of dog training have been so well systemized that it must be your fault, since literally thousands of fine Golden Retrievers have been trained by the book.

After your Golden Retriever is "letter perfect" under all conditions, then, if you wish, go on to advanced training and trick work.

Your Golden Retriever will love his obedience training, and you'll burst with pride at the finished product! Your Golden Retriever will enjoy life even more, and you'll enjoy your Golden Retriever more. And remember—*you owe good training to your Golden Retriever.*

Successful Dog Training is one of the better dog training books by Hollywood dog trainer Michael Kamer, who trains dogs for movie stars.

RETRIEVING

All retrievers are adapted by coat and nature to stand long, hard hours in a duck blind and retrieve wildfowl from icy water. Other breeds might retrieve ducks under moderate conditions but have no business being subjected to the icy elements on a typical duck day. Individuals of many breeds will take naturally to retrieving. Some mere puppies like to play with a ball and retrieve it. Some dogs will naturally retrieve the first bird ever killed in front of them. Some excellent retrievers have been just naturally developed. Equipment for teaching "force" retrieving consists of several "dummies" or objects to retrieve, a leash so that the dog will be under constant control and a slip or choke collar.

"Dummies" are made in varying forms. A piece of rubber hose about an inch in diameter and eight or ten inches long makes a good one. It is not too soft and is not injurious to the dog's teeth. A corncob is a simple dummy as clean ones are easily available, but they are rather soft for dogs inclined to be a bit hard-mouthed. A small bundle of turkey feathers is often used.

Before beginning the lessons, the trainer must decide on the method used to cause the dog to open his mouth. There are many ways to accomplish this. One way will work with one dog while another way will be more satisfactory with another dog. Squeezing a front paw gets results, others respond to a slight jerk on the choke collar. Find the most effective method for the individual and stick to it through his training.

Assuming your dog responds to the training collar, adjust it to his neck, with the running-free end on the upper side, and attach a short piece of stout cord. Grasp this up close to the ring with the right hand. Give the command "Fetch" in an ordinary tone of voice and accompany this command by a very slight jerk or

First and foremost a hunter, the Golden is always willing to go to retrieve game.

pressure on the collar. As the dog opens his mouth, instantly and gently place the dummy in it, slackening the pressure of the collar at the same moment. Hold your left hand under his mouth and thus keep it closed on the dummy. Soothe his fears and induce him to hold the dummy steadily, caressing him if he holds it well. The first lesson should not be too prolonged. After one or two repetitions, call it a day.

Continue with this first lesson regularly from day to day, until the dog will open his mouth promptly when you give the command "Fetch." Teach him to mouth it. These lessons should be given in a well-ventilated room, avoiding any distractions, diversions, or annoyances from spectators. A room has the further advantage of keeping the dog from cherishing ideas of escape, which may be his natural inclination during these early stages of training. In hot weather, the lessons should be given during the cool of early morning or late evening; under no circumstances should they be continued until the dog is

An eager to please Golden bringing in a pigeon at a fun trial.

manifestly discouraged under the restraint of discipline. Never end a lesson abruptly or with punishment. Lead the dog about for a few moments, praise and reassure him, then take off the training collar, thus concluding the lesson pleasantly.

Having taught the dog to open his mouth promptly to the order of "Fetch," the next stage is to teach him to step forward and grasp the object. In this lesson you need several feet of stout cord attached to the training collar so that the dog is free to step forward when he hears the order. Hold the dummy a few inches in front of the dog's mouth and on a level with it where he may both readily see and grasp it. Give the order "Fetch," exerting the necessary pressure on the collar at the same time and in a forward direction toward the dummy, thus assisting him to grasp it. The moment the dummy is in his mouth, the collar pressure must be slackened. Be deliberate, and praise the dog when he has done well. Continue with lessons in this manner until he will, without the pressure of the collar, step forward promptly

Returning a bird is fun work for the Golden Retriever; waiting for the command to retrieve is the tough part.

and grasp the dummy at the order of "Fetch."

At this juncture, the dog may continue holding the dummy when you wish him to release it, being apprehensive that, if it is not in his mouth, the pressure of the force collar may follow. Reassure him kindly every time he surrenders it to command. If he will not let go promptly upon order, grasp the end of the dummy in the left hand, but do not pull strongly on it. It is unwise to take it by direct force. When you have grasped the end of the dummy with your left hand, command him to "Give." Be prepared, if he refuses, to step lightly on the toes of his forefoot. Use just enough pressure on his foot to force him to open his mouth—and this will require but very little. After a few repetitions, he should surrender the dummy instantly upon the order to "Give."

If you twirl the dummy temptingly and playfully before the dog's nose he may attempt to grasp it. It is a distinct gain if he will do so. Then he can be taught in a few lessons to pick up the

Your Golden's most important goal in life is to please you. Remember to have time and patience while training to retrieve and you will be repaid ten-fold.

dummy. Too much playfulness should not be encouraged. The lessons must not lose the character of discipline. If too much playfulness is permitted, the force system will have no advantage over natural retrieving.

Having trained the dog so that he will step forward to grasp the dummy as ordered, the next stage is to teach him to lower his head to grasp it. This is accomplished simply by the process of gradually lowering the dummy at first only two or three inches at a time so that the change of position is not too sudden. You can tempt the dog with the dummy from the floor after a few attempts, particularly if you are tactful and do not proceed in too much of a hurry. A dog that is really anxious to please requires very little punishment and there may not be any perceptible stages in his progress; but in most instances the successive stages have to be formally and thoroughly observed. The dog requires time and schooling to comprehend his lessons. Hurrying him faster than he can comprehend or remember

Handler giving line to Golden Retriever.

simply results in loss of time in the end.

At last the dog will pick up the dummy when he is ordered to "Fetch," provided it is held on the floor; but if the hand is removed, he may at first make mistakes. He has previously been guided by following the hand. He may still follow the hand, which results in confusion if the hand is not near the dummy. By keeping the hand close to the dummy after it has been placed on the floor, the dog is induced to pick it up. Finally, after many repetitions, he should gradually forget the hand and learn to concentrate on the dummy alone.

It must be admitted that it is sometimes difficult to persuade certain dogs to lower their heads. Force is the only answer in such cases. You must compel obedience. This means that you must be firm. It does not mean that you must be rough.

After the dog will pick up the dummy you may next throw it a foot or two in front of him and give the order to "Fetch." In this lesson a longer check cord is required. If the dog does not move forward to the order, give him a pull to start him forward and at the same time repeat the order. If the previous stages of the training have been hurried over too rapidly, or imperfectly taught, the effect will be more manifest now than at any previous stage. It may even be necessary to return to some prior stage of development and begin all over again. If the dog has been properly prepared up to this point, it should be easy. This lesson should be thoroughly and regularly given, until the dog is reliably trained to fetch the object promptly without the use of the collar. Then he should be given practice on a dead bird.

When he can retrieve the dead bird well (which may require a number of special lessons) he may next be taken to the yard or even an open field for practice. Be sure that you have him under perfect control; for if the pupil once learns that he may escape from discipline by using his heels, you will but give yourself a new problem before the training in retrieving can proceed.

No slovenly disobedience should ever be accepted. Some men are satisfied if the dog brings the bird in and drops it close by. Do not accept such a performance. Insist that the dog completes his task. If you start slowly to walk away from him, this will often assist in inducing him to bring the bird in a direct line to you.

After your dog can fetch reliably, continue the lessons for

Your Golden will not hesitate to go into the water to retrieve—that's his specialty.

Waiting for his command, this Golden Retriever is demonstrating what a good retrieve is all about...obedience.

becomes an especially valuable trait later on in marking down game that falls to the gun.

He should be schooled to carry dead birds steadily to heel. You might shoot and drop a bird unobserved by the dog, but do it so that he will pass close and have a chance to smell it. Praise him highly if he picks it up. If he sniffs it but passes on you should pretend to find it yourself and your manner should give evidence of pleasure at discovering such a prize, so that the dog's interest and desire to emulate may be aroused. Then require the dog to retrieve it.

As mentioned before, always insist on a perfect retrieve to hand. If you have adopted the method of giving him rewards, do not permit him to hurry through

Carrying ever so gently so as not to ruffle any feathers, this Retriever is bringing home his charge.

many weeks so that the training will be indelibly imprinted upon his memory, and also to the end that perfect and prompt obedience may be established. He will then become so habituated to the work that disobedience or shirking never enters his mind.

In time, you may venture upon variations from the regular method, with a view to developing the dog's intelligence. The dummy may be shown to him and then thrown into bushes or tall grass, where he cannot see it, thereby forcing him to use his nose in finding it. The dog should learn to exercise a close watchfulness; this

his work or half do it in his eagerness to get the reward. Insist on having every detail properly observed. Nothing is more annoying in practical work than the dog's dropping a bird brought halfway in, or

INTRODUCTION TO WATER WORK

Most puppies of the Retriever breeds take naturally to water. Teaching the young dog to enter water is best accomplished in hot weather after he has had a good run and his body is heated. At

The retrieve is not complete until your Golden brings the bird back to your hand.

dropping the bird on the opposite side of a creek, necessitating a chase and retrieve on the part of the shooter, or another retrieve of the same bird by the dog.

Do not move when you send your dog in to retrieve game in the field. This is important. By tramping and stamping around in the vicinity of where you think the bird should be, you confuse your scent with that of the game you seek—and simply make it that much harder for the dog.

this time a stream or body of water will look tempting to him. Several young dogs together often make a "play-party" out of entering water and this gives the timid youngster more confidence.

As soon as the young dog learns to swim, the hardest part is over. He will enjoy his new-found accomplishment. An older dog, fond of swimming, will be a great aid. If he is not encouraged by the example of other dogs, it will be necessary to take a hand. This should be done carefully. Encourage him to wade out with

The best time to introduce your Golden Retreiver to water is when the weather is hot—it feels great!

you, or even go in swimming with you. Do not force him or frighten him as this may cause his fear to become exaggerated and permanent.

Once your dog is at home in the water, it should be a fairly easy matter to have him become an efficient retriever from water, provided he is already a force-trained retriever. At first, toss a bird or dummy for him close to the shore so that he will not have to swim for it. Repeat this several times, then increase the distance from shore until he has to swim for it. This may require some urging. Most young dogs are prone to step and shake themselves immediately upon

This bunch of Goldens is cooling off after an afternoon of fun.

The Golden Retriever is the epitome of a hearty sportsdog and hunter.

their return to shore, often dropping the retrieved object to do so. This should be discouraged promptly. If he picks up the object and brings it in to you, the offense is not so serious but it will be a mark against him in field trials. Insist on a prompt retrieve to hand at all times.

TAKING DIRECTIONS

The ability to take directions, or hand signals, promptly and correctly is a valuable accomplishment in any dog hunted in front of the gun, in the blind or heel as a non-slip retriever. Particularly valuable is it in a Spaniel or Retriever that has not seen the kill or properly marked the fall. These dogs should be taught to pause or look for directions immediately upon hearing several short blasts of the whistle.

When you have gained his attention in this manner, wave your hand in the direction you desire him to move and move yourself in that same direction. If you want him to "Go Back" wave your hand in a forward direction and move forward a little. If you want him to go to the right, wave your hand to the right and move to the right. The same applies to the left. If you want him to come closer to you, keep repeating the short blasts on the whistle and indicate your desire. By moving him in the direction desired, he will cross the line of scent and make the retrieve. The dog

should be allowed to use his own head as much as possible, and directions given only when necessary.

SOME NEVERS OF TRAINING

Never nag at a dog. When you speak to him, mean it. The dog constantly nagged at will never amount to much—and can't.

Never tease a dog. Respect him and earn his respect. Don't accept partial or slovenly performance. Insist that the dog completely perform any task as he has been taught he should.

Never vary commands. Always make them the same. Thus you preclude any confusion or uncertainty.

Never work or hunt your dog except with his equals or peers. If you go with men whose dogs will spoil yours, leave them and hunt alone—or if you go with them, don't take your dog.

Never lend your dog to anyone, not even a best friend—any more than you would your child. If you lend your dog to a friend the chances are you won't be friends for long.

Never ask anything unreasonable of a dog.

Never give him freedom to roam and find bad company. Dogs can get into bad habits the same as people.

Never let companions who hunt with you spoil the dog by breaking shot or otherwise. If a man breaks shot you can't blame a dog for doing so.

SHOWING YOUR GOLDEN

A show Golden Retriever is a comparatively rare thing. He is one out of several litters of puppies. He happens to be born with a degree of physical perfection that closely approximates the standard by which the breed is judged in the show ring. Such a dog should, on maturity, be able to win or approach his championship in good, fast company at the larger shows. Upon finishing his championship, he is apt to be as highly desirable as a breeding animal. As a proven stud, he will automatically command a high price for service.

Showing Golden Retrievers is a lot of fun—yes, but it is a highly competitive sport. While all the experts were once beginners, the odds are against a novice. You will be showing against experienced handlers, often people who have devoted a lifetime to breeding, picking the right ones, and then showing those dogs through to their championships. Moreover, the most perfect Golden Retriever ever born has faults, and in your hands the faults will be far more evident than with the experienced handler who knows how to minimize his Golden Retriever's faults. These are but a few points on the sad side of the picture.

The experienced handler, as I say, was not born knowing the ropes. He learned—*and so can you!* You can if you will put in the same time, study and keen observation that he did. But it will take time!

KEY TO SUCCESS

First, search for a truly fine show prospect. Take the puppy home, raise him by the book, and as carefully as you know how, give him every chance to mature into the Golden Retriever you hoped for. My advice is to keep your dog out of big shows, even

Showing your Golden Retriever is a very rewarding experience for you and your dog. You will see how your dog will love to perform in front of an audience.

Puppy Classes, until he is mature. Maturity in the male is generally two years; with the female, 14 months or so. When your Golden Retriever is approaching maturity, start out at match shows, and, with this experience for both of you, then go gunning for the big wins at the big shows.

Next step, read the standard by which the Golden Retriever is judged. Study it until you know it by heart. Having done this, and while your puppy is at home (where he should be) growing into a normal, healthy Golden Retriever, go to every dog show you can possibly reach. Sit at the ringside and watch Golden Retriever judging. Keep your ears and eyes open. Do your own judging, holding each of those dogs against the standard, which you now know by heart.

In your evaluations, don't start looking for faults. Look for the virtues—the best qualities. How does a given Golden Retriever shape up against the standard? Having looked for and noted the virtues, then note the faults and see what prevents a given Golden Retriever from standing correctly or moving well. Weigh these faults against the virtues, since, ideally, every feature of the dog should contribute to the harmonious whole dog.

If you plan on exhibiting your Golden Retriever, it is important that you purchase one that has real promise of becoming a fine show dog.

"RINGSIDE JUDGING"

It's a good practice to make notes on each Golden Retriever, always holding the dog against the standard. In "ringside judging," forget your personal preference for this or that feature. What does the standard say about it? Watch carefully as the judge places the dogs in a given class. It is difficult from the ringside always to see why number one was placed over the second dog. Try to follow the judge's reasoning. Later try to talk with the judge after he is finished. Ask him questions as to why he placed certain Golden Retrievers and not others. Listen while the judge explains his placings, and, I'll say right here, any judge worthy of his license should be able to give reasons.

When you're not at the ringside, talk with the fanciers who have Golden Retrievers. Don't be afraid to ask opinions or say that you don't know. You have a lot of listening to do, and it will help you a great deal and speed up your personal progress if you are a good listener.

There are different types of dog shows in which you may enter your Golden. In any show, it is important that you make sure your Golden Retriever is being presented to his best advantage.

THE NATIONAL CLUB

You will find it worthwhile to join the National Golden Retriever club and to subscribe to its magazine. From the national club, you will learn the location of an approved regional club near you. Now, when your young Golden Retriever is eight to ten months old, find out the dates of match shows in your section of the country. These differ from regular shows only in that no championship points are given. These shows are especially designed to launch young dogs (and new handlers) on a show career.

ENTER MATCH SHOWS

With the ring deportment you have watched at big shows firmly in mind and practice, enter your Golden Retriever in as many match shows as you can. When in the ring, you have two jobs. One is to see to it that your Golden Retriever is always being seen to its best advantage. The other job is to keep your eye on the judge to see what he may want you to do next. Watch only the judge and your Golden Retriever. Be quick and be alert; do exactly as the judge directs. Don't speak to him except to answer his questions. If he does something you don't like, don't say so. And don't irritate the judge (and everybody else) by constantly talking and fussing with your dog.

In moving about the ring, remember to keep clear of dogs beside you or in front of you. It is my advice to you *not* to show your Golden Retriever in a regular point show until he is at least close to maturity and after both you and your dog have had time to perfect ring manners and poise in the match shows.

Always be sure that you have fun with your Golden while at a show.

This Golden is demonstrating his gait at an outdoor show.

YOUR HEALTHY GOLDEN

We know our pets, their moods and habits, and therefore we can recognize when our Golden Retriever is experiencing an off-day. Signs of sickness can be very obvious or very subtle. As any mother can attest, diagnosing and treating an ailment require common sense, knowing when to seek home remedies and when to visit your doctor...or veterinarian, as the case may be.

Your veterinarian, we know, is your Golden Retriever's best friend, next to you. It will pay to be choosy about your veterinarian. Talk to dog-owning friends whom you respect. Visit more than one vet before you make a lifelong choice. Trust your instincts. Find a knowledgeable, compassionate vet who knows Golden Retrievers and likes them.

Grooming for good health

Your Golden's good health will show in his overall appearance. Bright eyes, a shiny coat and a kind expression are just some of the signs of a healthy dog.

makes good sense. The Golden's coat is double and medium in length. The dense outer coat benefits from regular brushing to keep it looking glossy and clean. Brushing stimulates the natural oils in the coat and also removes dead haircoat. Goldens shed seasonally, which means their undercoat (the soft downy white fur) is pushed out by the incoming new coat. A medium-strength bristle brush is all that is required to groom this beautiful breed of dog.

Anal sacs, sometimes called anal glands, are located in the musculature of the anal ring, one on either side. Each empties into the rectum via a small duct. Occasionally their secretion becomes thickened and accumulates so you can readily feel these structures from the outside. If your Golden Retriever is scooting across the floor dragging his rear quarters, or licking his rear, his anal sacs may need to be expressed. Placing pressure in and up toward the anus, while holding the tail, is the general routine. Anal sac secretions are characteristically foul-smelling, and you could get squirted if not careful. Veterinarians can take care of this during regular visits and demonstrate the cleanest method.

Many Golden Retrievers are predisposed to certain congenital and inherited abnormalities, such as hip dysplasia, a blatantly common problem in purebred dogs with few exceptions. Unfortunately, the Golden Retriever suffers from a high percentage rate of hip dysplasia despite the efforts of many conscientious breeders. This is due to the breed's unwavering popularity and the careless breeding that surrounds the procreation of such a popular breed. New owners must insist on screening certificates from such hip registries as OFA or PennHIP.

The Golden Retriever is an active breed, a natural athlete who needs solid construction to thrive. A new owner must insist on screening certificates from such hip registries as OFA or PennHIP.

Since HD is hereditary, it's necessary to know that the parents and grandparents of your puppy had hips rated good or better. Dysplastic dogs suffer from badly constructed hip joints which become arthritic and very painful, thereby hindering the dog's ability to be a working dog, a good-moving show dog, or even a happy, active pet.

Elbow dysplasia has recently become more of a concern, and the OFA screens for elbows as well. Young dogs typically show signs of limping or rotating elbows when walking or running, which may indicate that elbow dysplasia is present.

Osteochondritis dissecans affects the bones of many large breeds, and although many other breeds are more prone to this disease, the Golden Retriever has been a victim on many occasions. Panosteitis, affecting bone production, as well as hypertrophic osteodystrophy and myasthenia gravis are also reported as potential bone

Because he is such an important member of the family, the aging Golden Retriever's health should be monitored carefully. Any sudden change in appetite or activity level should be relayed to your veterinarian.

diseases in the Golden.

Eye conditions such as pannus, cataracts, retinal dysplasia, and progressive retinal atrophy have become concerns for Golden breeders. Screening for eye problems has therefore been prioritized. Bilateral cataracts are the most frequently seen in Golden Retrievers, and retinal dysplasia, more common than PRA, is an inherited defect that can severely reduce a dog's vision. Entropion and ectropion, both affecting the eyelids, affect Goldens, as does distichiasis (extra eyelashes). All of these can be corrected through surgery, though eliminate the dog from competing in dog shows.

A well-bred Golden Retriever is a healthy, long-lived companion animal.

Von Willebrand's disease, a bleeding disorder, and Hemophilia A are conditions that affect many dog breeds and do not exclude the Golden Retriever.

Certain heart conditions, such as patent or persistent ductus arteriosus and persistent right aortic arch, are concerns in the Golden Retriever, though not frequently encountered. More common in Goldens is SAS, subvalvular aortic stenosis, which is manifest in a heart murmur. SAS is considered hereditary and affected dogs should not be bred.

Epilepsy, a possible hereditary condition that is linked to the brain's receiving incorrect stimulus, hinders many breeds of dog and is problematic in Goldens. Affected dogs show signs of mild seizures between six months and three years. Although incurable, fits can be treated with medication.

Hypothyroidism (malfunction of the thyroid gland) can be linked to many symptoms in Goldens, such as obesity, lethargy, and reproductive disorders. Supplementation of the thyroid decreases problems, though such dogs should likely not be bred.

Despite this lengthy list of potential problems, a well-bred

Every dog naps from time to time, however, excessive napping or listlessness could be a sign that your Golden is not feeling well.

Golden is a healthy, long-lived companion animal. Proper care and education can only help owners promote the health and longevity of their dogs. Most breeders advise against feeding the Golden Retriever one large meal per day because of the dangers of bloat (gastric torsion), the twisting of the stomach causes gas to build up and the organ expands like a balloon. Avoiding strenuous exercise and large amounts of water can preclude the occurrence of bloat, as can feeding two smaller meals instead of one larger one. A good commercial dog food is recommended for the dog's balanced diet.

For the continued health of your dog, owners must attend to vaccinations regularly. Your veterinarian can recommend a vaccination schedule appropriate for your dog, taking into consideration the factors of climate and geography. The basic vaccinations to protect your dog are: parvovirus, distemper, hepatitis, leptospirosis, adenovirus, parainfluenza, coronavirus, bordetella, tracheobronchitis (kennel cough), Lyme disease and rabies.

Parvovirus is a highly contagious, dog-specific disease, first recognized in 1978. Targeting the small intestine, parvo affects the stomach, and diarrhea and vomiting (with blood) are clinical signs. Although the dog can pass

Keeping your Golden's ears clean is simple if you use a top-quality lotion. It is essential that you maintain your dog's ears, claws, mouth and fur. Photo courtesy of Hagen.

ultimately in the nervous system and epithelial tissues. Young dogs or dogs with weak immune systems can develop encephalomyelitis (brain disease) from the distemper infection. Such dogs experience seizures, general weakness and rigidity, as well as "hardpad." Since distemper is largely incurable, prevention through vaccination is vitally important. Puppies should be vaccinated at six to eight weeks of age, with boosters at ten to 12 weeks. Older puppies (16 weeks and older) who are unvaccinated should receive no fewer than two vaccinations at three- to four-week intervals.

Hepatitis mainly affects the liver and is caused by canine adenovirus type I. Highly infectious, hepatitis often affects dogs nine to 12 months of age. Initially the virus localizes in the dog's tonsils and then disperses to the liver, kidney and eyes. Generally speaking the dog's immune system is capable of combating this virus. Canine infectious hepatitis affects dogs whose systems cannot fight off the adenovirus. Affected dogs have fever, abdominal pains, bruising on mucous membranes and gums, and experience comas and convulsions. Prevention of hepatitis exists only through vaccination at eight to ten weeks of age and then boosters three or four weeks later, then annually.

Leptospirosis is a bacterium-related disease, often spread by rodents. The organisms that spread leptospirosis enter through the mucous membranes and

the infection to other dogs within three days of infection, the initial signs, which include lethargy and depression, don't display themselves until four to seven days. When affecting puppies under four weeks of age, the heart muscle is frequently attacked. When the heart is affected, the puppies exhibit difficulty in breathing and experience crying and foaming at the nose and mouth.

Distemper, related to human measles, is an airborne virus that spreads in the blood and spread to the internal organs via the bloodstream. It can be passed through the dog's urine. Leptospirosis does not affect young dogs as consistently as do the other viruses; it is reportedly regional in distribution and somewhat dependent on the immunostatus of the dog. Fever, inappetence, vomiting, dehydration, hemorrhage, kidney and eye disease can result in moderate cases.

Bordetella, called canine cough, causes a persistent hacking cough in dogs and is very contagious. Bordetella involves a virus and a bacteria: parainfluenza is the most common virus implicated; *Bordetella bronchiseptica,* the bacterium. Bronchitis and pneumonia result in less than 20 percent of the cases, and most dogs recover from the condition within a week to four weeks. Non-prescription medicines can help relieve the hacking cough, though nothing can cure the condition before it's run its course. Vaccination cannot guarantee protection from canine cough, but it does ward off the most common virus responsible for the condition.

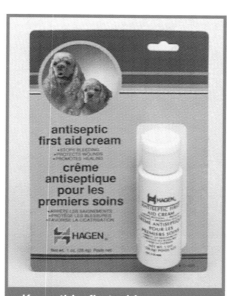

antiseptic first aid cream
•STOPS BLEEDING
•PROTECTS WOUNDS
•PROMOTES HEALING

crème antiseptique pour les premiers soins
•ARRÊTE LES SAIGNEMENTS
•PROTÈGE LES BLESSURES
•FAVORISE LA CICATRISATION

HAGEN

Keep this first aid cream on hand in cases of scrapes and cuts as it is antiseptic. Photo courtesy of Hagen.

Lyme disease (also called borreliosis), although known for decades, was only first diagnosed in dogs in 1984. Lyme disease can affect cats, cattle, and horses, but especially people. In the US, the disease is transmitted by two ticks carrying the *Borrelia burgdorferi* organism: the deer tick (*Ixodes scapularis*) and the western black-legged tick (*Ixodes pacificus*), the latter primarily affects reptiles. In Europe, *Ixodes ricinus* is responsible for spreading Lyme. The disease causes lameness, fever, joint swelling, inappetence, and lethargy. Removal of ticks from the dog's coat can help reduce the chances of Lyme, though not as much as avoiding heavily wooded areas where the dog is most likely to contract ticks. A vaccination is available, though it has not been proven to protect dogs from all strains of the organism that causes the disease.

Rabies is passed to dogs and people through wildlife: in North America, principally through the skunk, fox and raccoon; the bat is not the culprit it was once thought to be. Likewise, the common image of the rabid dog foaming at the mouth with every

Excessive scratching could be an indication that your Golden has fleas. Be sure to thoroughly check your dog after a walk outside.

for centuries. Despite our modern efforts, fleas still pester our pet's existence, and our own. All dogs itch, and fleas can make even the happiest dog a miserable, scabby mess. The loss of hair and habitual biting and chewing at themselves rank among the annoyances; the nuisances include the passing of tapeworms and the whole family's itching through the summer months. A full range of flea-control and elimination products are available at pet shops, and your veterinarian surely has recommendations. Sprays, powders, collars and dips fight fleas from the outside; drops and pills fight the good fight from inside. Discuss the possibilities with your vet. Not all products

hair on end is unlikely the truest scenario. A rabid dog exhibits difficulty eating, salivates much and has spells of paralysis and awkwardness. Before a dog reaches this final state, it may experience anxiety, personality changes, irritability and more aggressiveness than is usual. Vaccinations are strongly recommended as rabid dogs are too dangerous to manage and are commonly euthanized. Puppies are generally vaccinated at 12 weeks of age, and then annually. Although rabies is on the decline in the world community, tens of thousands of humans die each year from rabies-related incidents.

Parasites have clung to our pets

Should he become infested with fleas and ticks, your Golden Retriever will have to be bathed with a good medicated shampoo made especially for him. Photo courtesy of Hagen.

A family that plays together is a family that stays together. Fleas and ticks can also affect family members and cause a problem within the home.

can be used in conjunction with one another, and some dogs may be more sensitive to certain applications than others. The dog's living quarters must be debugged as well as the dog itself. Heavy infestation may require multiple treatments.

Always check your dog for ticks carefully. Although fleas can be acquired almost anywhere, ticks are more likely to be picked up in heavily treed areas, pastures or other outside grounds (such as dog shows or obedience or field trials). Athletic, active, and hunting dogs are the most likely subjects, though any passing dog can be the host. Remember Lyme disease is passed by tick infestation.

As for internal parasites, worms are potentially dangerous for dogs and people. Roundworms,

Golden Retrievers have captured the hearts of millions of people with their award winning dispositions and overall good looks.

hookworms, whipworms, tapeworms, and heartworms comprise the blightsome party of troublemakers. Deworming puppies begins at around two to three weeks and continues until three months of age. Proper hygienic care of the environment is also important to prevent procedures with your veterinarian.

Roundworms pose a great threat to dogs and people. They are found in the intestine of dogs and can be passed to people through ingestion of feces-contaminated dirt. Roundworm infection can be prevented by not

Although your Golden doesn't require his own meadow to stay content, what a way to spend a lazy afternoon.

contamination with roundworm and hookworm eggs. Heartworm preventatives are recommended by most veterinarians, although there are some drawbacks to the regular introduction of poisons into our dogs' systems. These daily or monthly preparations also help regulate most other worms as well. Discuss worming walking dogs in heavy-traffic people areas, by burning feces, and by curbing dogs in a responsible manner. (Of course, in most areas of the country, curbing dogs is the law.) Roundworms are typically passed from the bitch to the litter, and bitches should be treated along with the puppies, even if she

The picture of good health and happiness—a Golden puppy, a fuzzy kitten and flowers from a friend—who could ask for more?!

tested negative prior to whelping. Generally puppies are treated every two weeks until two months of age.

Hookworms, like roundworms, are also a danger to dogs and people. The hookworm parasite (known as *Ancylostoma caninum*) causes cutaneous larva migrans in people. The eggs of hookworms are passed in feces and become infective in shady, sandy areas. The larvae penetrate the skin of the dog, and the dog subsequently becomes infected. When swallowed, these parasites affect the intestines, lungs, windpipe, and the whole digestive system. Infected dogs suffer from anemia and lose large amounts of blood in the places where the worms latch onto the dog's intestines, etc.

Although infrequently passed to humans, whipworms are cited as one of the most common parasites in America. These elongated worms affect the intestines of the dog, where they latch on, and cause colic upset or diarrhea. Unless identified in stools passed, whipworms are difficult to diagnose. Adult worms can be eliminated more consistently than the larvae, since whipworms exhibit unusual life cycles. Proper hygienic care of outdoor grounds is critical to the avoidance of these harmful parasites.

Tapeworms are carried by fleas, and enter the dog when the dog

Chewing on wood can be dangerous for your Golden, as he can swallow pieces and splinters can lodge in his throat. Provide your Golden Retriever with safe chew toys to avoid this situation.

Goldens and their children can be any shade of lustrous gold—even blonde!

swallows the flea. Humans can acquire tapeworms in the same way, though we are less likely to swallow fleas than dogs are. Recent studies have shown that certain rodents and other wild animals have been infected with tapeworms, and dogs can be affected by catching and/or eating these other animals. Of course, outdoor hunting dogs and terriers are more likely to be infected in this way than are your typical house dog or non-motivated hound. Treatment for tapeworm has proven very effective, and infected dogs do not show great discomfort or symptoms. When people are infected, however, the liver can be seriously damaged. Proper cleanliness is the best bet against tapeworms.

Heartworm disease is transmitted by mosquitoes and badly affects the lungs, heart and blood vessels of dogs. The larvae of *Dirofilaria immitis* enters the dog's bloodstream when bitten by an infected mosquito. The larvae takes about six months to mature. Infected dogs suffer from weight loss, appetite loss, chronic coughing and general fatigue. Not all affected dogs show signs of illness right away, and carrier dogs may be affected for years before clinical signs appear. Treatment of heartworm disease has been effective but can be dangerous also. Prevention as always is the desirable alternative. Ivermectin is the active ingredient in most heartworm preventatives and has proven to be successful. Check with your veterinarian for the preparation that is best for your dog. Dogs generally begin taking the preventatives at eight months of age and continue to do so throughout the non-winter months.

SUGGESTED READING

The following books are all published by T.F.H. Publications and are recommended to you for additional information:

Everybody Can Train Their Own Dog by Angela White (TW-113) is a fabulous reference guide for all dog owners. This well written, easy-to-understand book covers all training topics in alphabetical order for instant location. In addition to teaching, this book provides problem solving and problem prevention techniques that are fundamental to training. All teaching methods are based on motivation and kindness, which bring out the best of a dog's natural ability and instinct.

Dog Breeding for Professionals by Dr. Herbert Richards (H-969) is a straightforward discussion of how to breed dogs of various sizes

and how to care for newborn puppies. The many aspects of breeding (including possible problems and practical solutions) are covered in great detail. Warning: the explicit photos of canine sexual activities may offend some readers.

The Atlas of Dog Breeds of the World (H-1091) by Bonnie Wilcox, DVM, and Chris Walkowicz traces the history and highlights the characteristics, appearance and function of every recognized dog breed in the world. 409 different breeds receive full-color treatment and individual study. Hundreds of breeds in addition to those recognized by the American Kennel Club and the Kennel Club of Great Britain are included—the dogs of the world complete! The